2018. First edition. Unabridged.

Cover design: Verlag Kunst und Kapitalismus.
Photo: Ciara Spurling
Verlag Kunst und Kapitalismus.
First Edition. Unabridged.
Copyright © F.T. Spurling, 2018.
All rights reserved.
Production and publishing: BoD- Books on Demand
Norderstedt, Germany
ISBN 9783752857696

...NOT QUITE

F.T. SPURLING

Verlag Kunst und Kapitalismus
zu Berlin

Contents

I have no money, no resources, no hopes.
I am the happiest man alive.

-Henry Miller

**let's talk about bondage
and the fact that I'm a little forward**

sick and full of love that floats with the bank
down a glass river into rusted nights,
mornings which become mornings, with tales of other
mornings that are impossible.

rotating with eyes that look like they want
sicking beds of laptops and cords, unstuck sheets and yeah
the vision of the world torn edited for a 17" screen.
shear breaths. panic wringing of arms for some far off banker maybe,
the such is what's asked for,

"YEAH VISIONS OF WORDS TORN" and their seats, and their
tables. 1.20 beers stuck in coats of torn cigars and wrappers
drenched in the cleanness of grease. jamming on each other forgetting
to puke, and "fuck isn't it so cheap". "they don't even bother to check
after 9; open all weekend". what time is a weekend apart from
yesterday?

Still pull and get static. flung through plate glass,
dance unbloodied with a smile that knows the
bladder is full and that so
what if the job the next day is a loan

and maybe the next and "maybe" it will be winter again,
feet with snow and credit flung without a ring. it's found
we find and there is painting of the lips, mine are mirrors.

taxis, tarmac, abandoned streets, white is the distance,
tacked and clean, ornate, forgotten. we pour out,
tumbling, chairs break, falling into bikes, pool tables.
hands in inappropriate public places with shouts going
in. bad writing and dance, dance and what's left to strip bare,
crack of the ash, green going thin.

the haze left was as popular, as burdened, as electric, as some
ghost which has left the shelter of a smelted history to breathe, eat,
yet again before its idea is tapped for sale like before. desolate with
music, doors swing with something of a beat. ground unburied
and what is in the air above the dropped hands sees for miles, which are
incomprehensible with its vision.

...Not Quite.

F.T. Spurling

...Not Quite.

bench

because of who I lay
my fingers,
cast them into the
tangles,
I can feel my bones
become like oil
across water
floating the surface,
unable to go
any deeper

...Not Quite.

**cracked glass
and the humorous spilling of**

never really understood,
(not meant to)
keep smiling,
down with cocked
simplicity,
open to jabbering on
mute,
Hang onto the
slicked grain,
laugh to
the crowd
-Yelling
pouring ash on
chins-
settling into
Plans
Pre-sets
complex mumbles,
(You could)
Wake up,
on these billion
tapped planks,

Make for the
door,
drip nicotine,
slip
Past the mouth,
Strait to the
hip, Easy,
but, wait...
Maybe
just
for a
split
(near end of sorts)
second
"go on"
Keep your head up,
Shout an Order,
fall
back, and
blur in the
night

...Not Quite.

...Not Quite.

down to a hall of phosphorescence

our backs are forward,
I stare at straps, white darker
than cotton,

each step deliberate,
heads forward, leaving to
know a direction,

your black cascade holds up,
the tones become faint
traces,

we smell of cigarettes, rolled
out of deep exchanges
and horse shit,

which after the corner are similar.
this refuses to be an issue,
entering silence

...Not Quite.

4/4

heads down/hands up,
hands down/heads up, eyes
shut to sweat, breath in a
break,

tendencies like hips
which become 7AM, with the
floor emptying, as writhing.
being the same way

a step
back but steep,
words working on pure syllables,
garbled paragons that have been
kind of understood.

given the excuses and the
excess. stepping into the rain
still dark in day,
dry of detail
ears sing their death above
taxis, each step heavy light

...Not Quite.

...Not Quite.

TOR

taking of what was left from the crumpled
pack, light, white while
pulling memory to the floor.
between the bricks where we wound our time,
there becomes a lack of denial which
is wanted, speeches on moving on,
of getting there.

you're parked, locked up, two left,
my bullshit has gone thin,
still kissing him I can feel the what the fuck
from your side, wanting it to be your
dressed hip,

but we are humming beneath the
music. I'd like to skip dancing,
to start giving a break but my lungs,
each bit of inhale tearing like the advice
that comes deep with
tiredness,

which hasn't even started to get on with going
deaf. running into concrete, my feet
clawed by few hands,
both are slipping in the torrents holding
stiff, empty in light pollution with a
blank cardboard chest below.

yet getting back, I'm convinced you're standing
naked beside the bed, hands cocked unseen
in the soft-core of my time

...Not Quite.

...Not Quite.

heartless

find yourself lost on
a night before it falls,
seeing how you keep pushing
mistakes, with knowledge
that you've won,

jaunted anger going ways
that come back,
pushed with better ways,
spilled advice to keep to the
line, while your head fits
on the block with a smile

which makes it sort of worse,
up in the morning light,
breath cold in the room,
winning on the end of
it, arguments with the cash that
goes,

placing resolve to your hands,
normality keeping pace, feeling
that the victory will get bigger,
with populations getting wider,

voice so fucking loud with
a little grit in it

...Not Quite.

...Not Quite.

reiterating

pursuit of my eyes,
which keep bleeding
as they turn to dust,

you learn to lean into
corners, making wax
seem permanent,

I am blind asking you
to get up, maybe help to
a door,

caring enough, that
want of warm air,

while you shake
a skirt, heavy
as wood into the
distance

F.T. Spurling

...Not Quite.

morning, midwinter, Rixdorf

things kept, kept destroyed,
tossed or put piles
gather dust, sentimentality;

tickets
outbound for buses covered in
dirt snow, a goodbye for a friend,

crisp packets, hungover cigarettes
shared, backyards on glass,
looking up,

chipped paint
on old windows, faint music going
from the night before,

bottles of paradise with cuts along the rims
shooting for refunds, cents worth more
than what went down

or spat twisting out
between the space, begging for seconds
longer,

shit in shit out, a collection of age that
keeps gathering, bits lost of meaning
their presence feels on the
hand,

like stones, far broken from
what strength they could carry aside
what they make in a fist to crack,

a moment

...Not Quite.

F.T. Spurling

...Not Quite.

F.T. Spurling is Irish, Canadian. His poetry has been published in Australia, Derry and Germany.

He has lived in Berlin since 2011, where he has tried to live a quiet life.

...Not Quite.

www.kunstundkapitalismus.com

...Not Quite.

set the lake on fire